Easy Classic Tunes for Clarinet

Piano Accompaniment

Arranged by Stephen Duro

Amsco Publications
New York/London/Sydney

CD track listing

1   **Tuning note (A)**

Full instrumental performances:

2   **March** (Handel)

3   **Poor Wand'ring One** (Sullivan)

4   **Barcarolle** (Offenbach)

5   **Skaters' Waltz** (Waldteufel)

6   **Theme from The New World Symphony** (Dvořák)

7   **Air On The G String** (Bach)

8   **Basse-Danse** (Warlock)

9   **Pavane** (Fauré)

10 **Say Goodbye Now To Pastime** (Mozart)

11 **O For The Wings Of A Dove** (Mendelssohn)

12 **Toreador's Song** (Bizet)

Backing tracks only:

13 **March** (Handel)

14 **Poor Wand'ring One** (Sullivan)

15 **Barcarolle** (Offenbach)

16 **Skaters' Waltz** (Waldteufel)

17 **Theme from The New World Symphony** (Dvořák)

18 **Air On The G String** (Bach)

19 **Basse-Danse** (Warlock)

20 **Pavane** (Fauré)

21 **Say Goodbye Now To Pastime** (Mozart)

22 **O For The Wings Of A Dove** (Mendelssohn)

23 **Toreador's Song** (Bizet)

Music processed by Allegro Reproductions
Cover design by Ian Butterworth
Cover photograph by Ron Sutherland

This book Copyright © 1999 by Amsco Publications,
A Division of Music Sales Corporation, New York

Order No. AM 961895
International Standard Book Number: 0.8256.1777.4

Exclusive Distributors:
Music Sales Corporation
257 Park Avenue South, New York, NY 10010 USA

Printed in the United States of America by
Vicks Lithograph and Printing Corporation

Contents

MARCH
from Scipione

By George Friderick Handel

Triumphantly

POOR WAND'RING ONE

from The Pirates Of Penzance

Music by Arthur Sullivan

Moderately bright

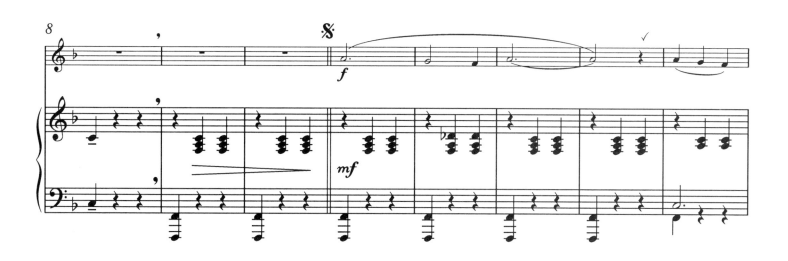

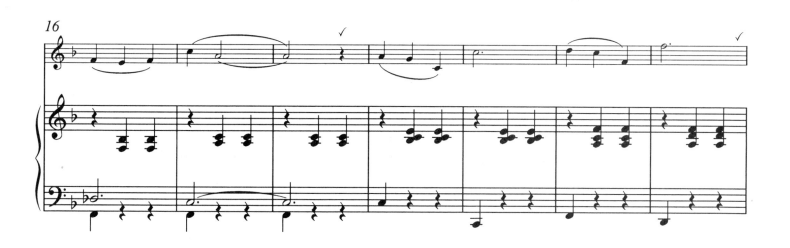

BARCAROLLE

from The Tales Of Hoffmann

By Jacques Offenbach

Moderately

SKATERS' WALTZ

By Emile Waldteufel

In brilliant style

Moderately

THEME FROM THE NEW WORLD SYMPHONY

By Anton Dvořák

Easy Classic Tunes for Clarinet

Clarinet part

Arranged by Stephen Duro

Amsco Publications
New York/London/Sydney

MARCH
from Scipione

By George Friderick Handel

Triumphantly

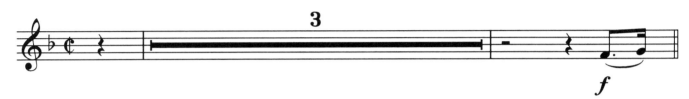

3

POOR WAND'RING ONE

from The Pirates Of Penzance

Music by Arthur Sullivan

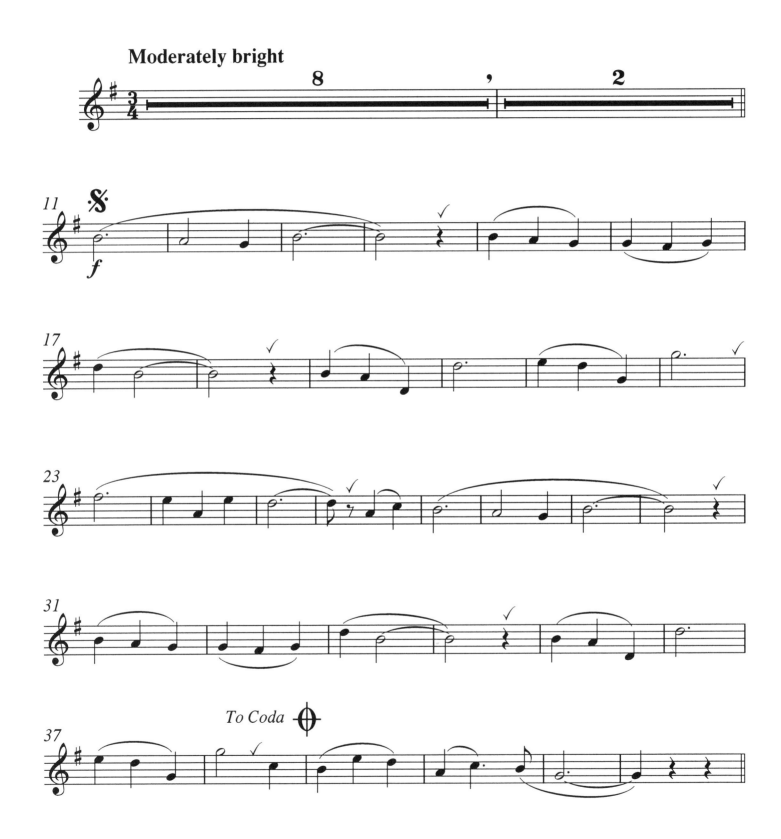

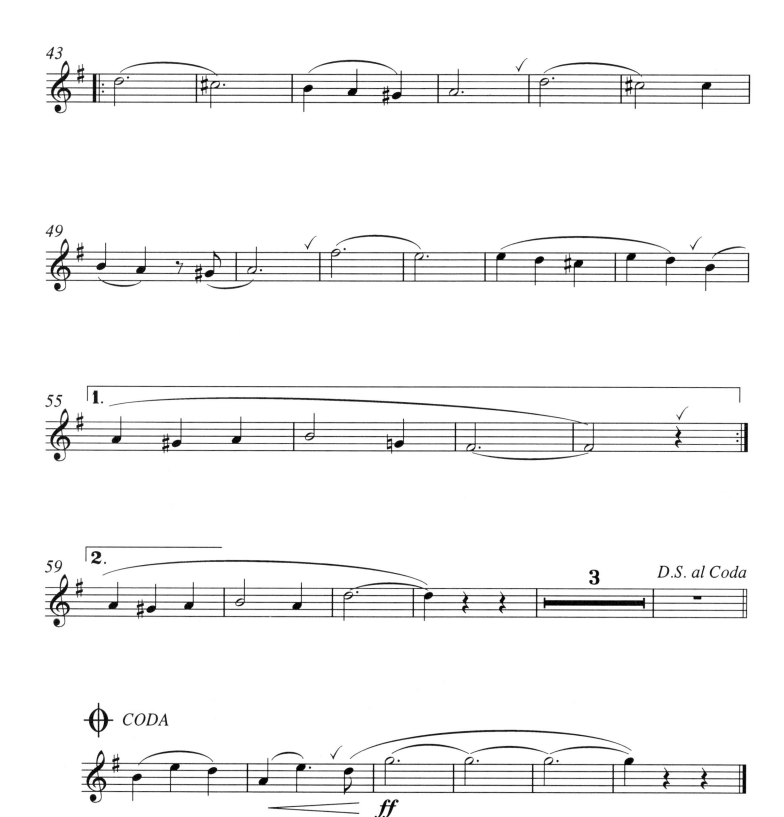

BARCAROLLE
from The Tales Of Hoffmann

By Jacques Offenbach

SKATERS' WALTZ

By Emile Waldteufel

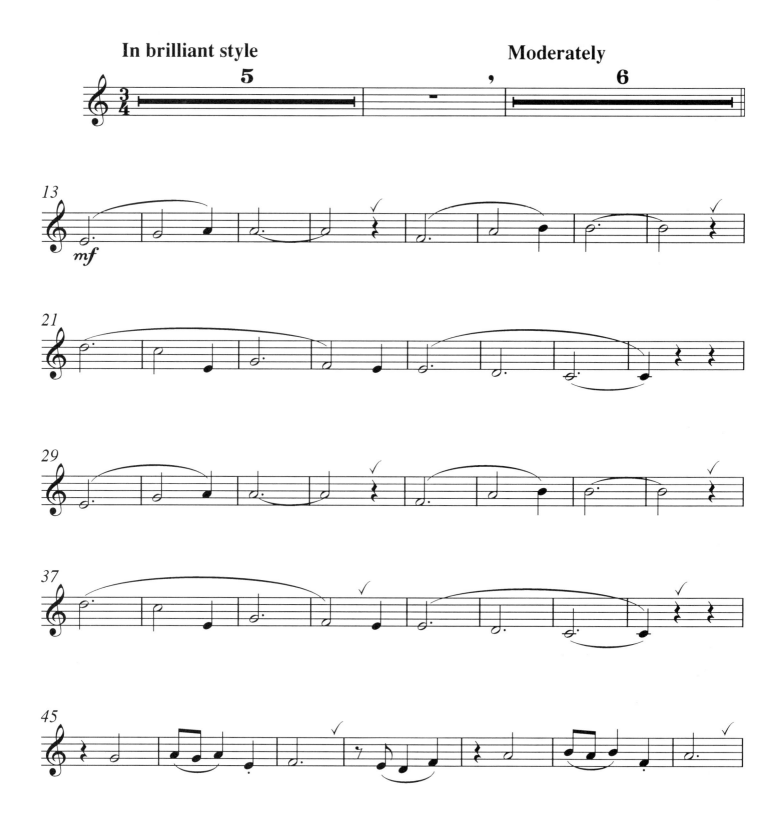

THEME FROM
THE NEW WORLD SYMPHONY

By Anton Dvořák

Slow

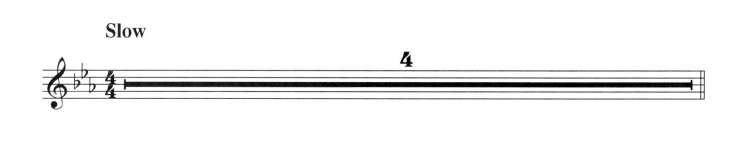

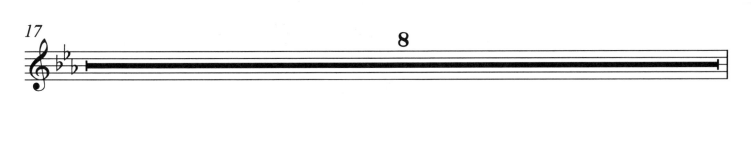

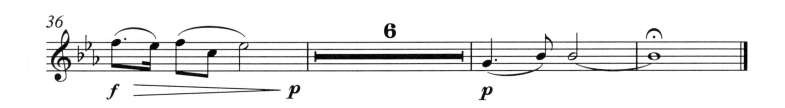

AIR ON THE G STRING
from Orchestral Suite in D

By Johann Sebastian Bach

Moderately slow

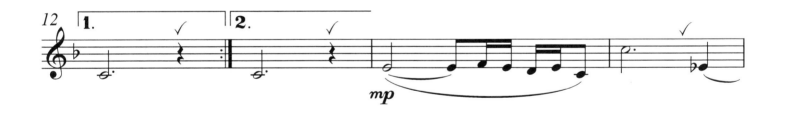

crescendo   poco   a   poco

f

BASSE-DANSE

from Capriol Suite

By Peter Warlock

PAVANE

By Gabriel Fauré

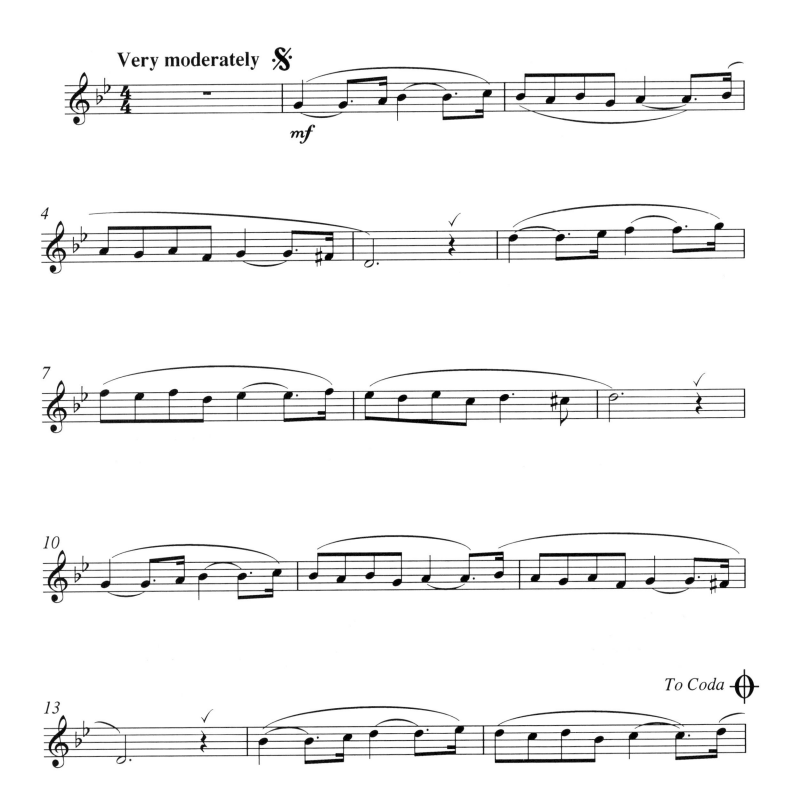

D.S. al Coda

CODA **molto rit.**

SAY GOODBYE NOW TO PASTIME
from The Marriage Of Figaro
by Wolfgang Amadeus Mozart

O FOR THE WINGS OF A DOVE

from Hear My Prayer

By Felix Mendelssohn-Bartholdy

TOREADOR'S SONG
from Carmen

By Georges Bizet

Contents

This book © Copyright 1999 by Amsco Publications, A Division of Music Sales Corporation
Order No. AM 961895 ISBN 0.8256.1777.4

AIR ON THE G STRING

from Orchestral Suite in D

By Johann Sebastian Bach

Moderately slow

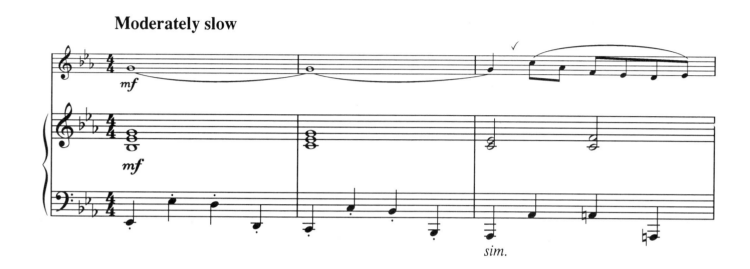

22

BASSE-DANSE

from Capriol Suite

By Peter Warlock

Moderately bright

PAVANE

By Gabriel Fauré

D.S. al Coda

CODA

molto rit.

SAY GOODBYE NOW TO PASTIME

from The Marriage Of Figaro

by Wolfgang Amadeus Mozart

Moderately bright

32

O FOR THE WINGS OF A DOVE

from Hear My Prayer

By Felix Mendelssohn-Bartholdy

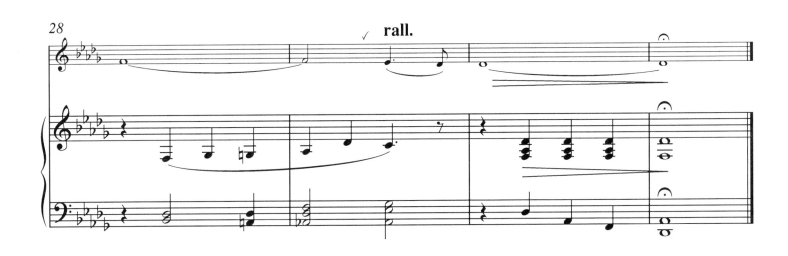

TOREADOR'S SONG

from Carmen

By Georges Bizet